Your Business Shouldn't Need You

Start to Replace Yourself in 180 Days

PETER COX

Your Business Shouldn't Need You: Start to Replace Yourself in 180 Days ©
Peter Cox 2020

ISBN: 978-1-925962-99-4 (paperback)

Millionaire Maker Series: Book One

Published in Australia by Peter Cox, InHouse Publishing, and GOKO Publishing.
www.leadershipdynamics.com.au
www.inhousepublishing.com.au

Printed in Australia by InHouse Print & Design.

Contents

Dedications ix

Acknowledgements xi

Introduction xiii

Chapter 1: Being Led 1

Chapter 2: Growing Your Influence 13

Chapter 3: Casting Vision 23

Chapter 4: Setting Clear Expectations. 35

Chapter 5: Building Team Culture 43

Chapter 6: Growing Unity. 59

Summing Up. 71

"I have worked with Peter Cox since the early 2000s and more so over the past decade. I've taken the leadership principles taught by Peter as well as the practical real-life examples, and I've embedded those in the organisations and teams I work with. It is a privilege to partner closely with Peter on a global basis with Leadership Dynamics to impact the world for good."

*— **Tony Davis, Founder, Chairman and CEO of Companies and NPOs, Dovetail Business Solutions, The Advisory Boards, Adavise, The Cancer Lifeboat, Medsquirrel***

"Peter Cox worked with the Manly NRL football team from 2005 to 2011. In that time, Peter coordinated and delivered a leadership-based and thinking strategy. It enlightened and promoted clear vision under which the players learned to deal with times of adversity both on and off the football field. The players and staff were enriched by the experiences that Peter provided.

During his seven-year tenure, the Manly NRL team qualified for the NRL finals seven years in a row; qualified for three grand finals; and won two NRL premierships in 2008 and 2011. The team was well regarded by the brand of football they played. No doubt, a significant part was the visualisation provided by Peter Cox."

*— **Des Hasler, Head Coach, Manly Sea Eagles NRL Team***

Dedications

To my wonderful parents, Dad and Mum, Brian and Claire, who celebrated 60 years of marriage in July 2019, and who always led by example, providing for my sister, Jacqueline, and me. My parents instilled deep values into me and as I get older, I reminisce about the difficult times we had as a family and how our values kept us together, and I'll be forever grateful for the sacrifices they made to give us the opportunities we've had in our lives.

To my beautiful wife, Debbie (Boo Boo), who has been with me since we first met on Great Keppel Island, the Great Barrier Reef, on December 11, 1985. Married for 32 years, together for 35 years so far. Without Deb I would not be able to do what I do today, and I would not be the man I am today without her inspiring me to be the very best version of myself, which has resulted in my leadership constantly growing and reaching higher levels. Thank you, Deb, for everything you do and for the wonderful mum you are for our two sons, Dane and Jarrod. Behind every great man is a better woman.

To my special sons, Dane (26) and Jarrod (24). I will always have your back and I will always lead you to keep climbing. Life is not easy at times and it certainly is not fair, which my mentor, Jim, taught me in 1992 when I thought I was a big shot at 29 years of age. I will always be in your corner, Dane and Jarrod. Time passes quickly, so make the most of your life each day and surround yourself with wise people – be led.

To the two closest confidants I had in my life, who both passed away within four weeks of each other, in July and August 2013 – Jim, my mentor, and Boris, one of my closest friends who was so dear to me – may you both rest in peace and just know the huge, positive impact you both had on Coxey's life for different reasons. There's not one day that goes by that I don't think of each of you. It was the first time in my life I suffered real loss and it was devastating. It humbled me and made me realise the importance of the leadership principles I learnt from both of you, which I pass on to anybody that truly wants to grow in leadership. Thank you, brothers.

Acknowledgements

To my Leadership Dynamics team – Christine Chandler, 29 years as my P.A., has continued to keep climbing the mountain with me, having started our first business in my garage in Sylvania, Southern Sydney, in 1991. Without you, Christine, everything that has happened on this leadership journey would not have been possible. Your loyalty, your professionalism and your beautiful heart and spirit I hold dear to my heart and I'll always be there for you and Ian and your two sons, Mark and Andrew.

To Kylie Francesconi, the Marketing Manager of Leadership Dynamics, who has professionally assisted me in writing this book and growing my brand across many platforms and countries – you continue to amaze me with your heart and spirit and your servanthood leadership. It humbles me and makes me very grateful because I cannot do what I'm doing without you beside me. Keep growing and believing in yourself because you're not the Kylie I started with, and now look where we're going. Keep climbing with me and don't look back.

To all my global partners and clients, without your trust in me, this book would not be possible. I'll continue to be the very best leader I can be for all of you and for the people I haven't met yet who are going to come into my life, so that I can keep building you into stronger leaders and help you live better lives.

To the professional sporting coaches and players whose lives I've had the honour and privilege to be a part of – I will always treasure and value what I've learnt from being part of the inner circle in a high-performance team; being able to utilise my Leadership Dynamics process to grow people and culture in your team environment; and to scale to the very top of the mountain, at times – "the Holy Grail".

Introduction

When I started my first business in 1988, my leadership mentor, Jim, was a very successful global entrepreneur running a $100 million+ business. He led me for 22 years before he passed in July 2013. Jim taught me the life-changing lesson that my business shouldn't need me; that it shouldn't be reliant on me to function. Jim taught me that I needed to replace myself, so that my business didn't own me.

Replacing yourself doesn't mean you're out of your business, nor does it mean you have to sell your business, but what it does mean is having a deliberate process in place where the business can operate and grow with or without you, if you choose.

It's a personal choice you can make, because you can. You can spend as much or as little time as you like on the business because you've raised up skilled leaders around you to share the responsibility of leading and running your business in a thriving and empowering environment.

Thirty-one years later, I continue to ensure that this lesson, and the key strategies and principles I'll outline in this book, which form part of my Leadership Dynamics process, are adopted and upheld within my businesses, and also for my clients who implement my process alongside their own, as I've experienced first-hand just how powerful these strategies and principles are. The Replacement Principle and my Leadership Dynamics process were key strategic components to successfully expanding one of our businesses into 28 countries by the year 2006.

My Leadership Dynamics process has continued to grow and add tremendous value to all my clients since its launch in 2003. *They are, as I like to say, all LEADING4GROWTH, because if you're not growing then you're going to stay where you are!*

As you go through the leadership journey of this book, there are many testimonials that will add credibility to the Leadership Dynamics process. You'll note that the testimonials are from business owners and professional sporting coaches, as well as their key leaders, demonstrating that the leadership strategies and principles I will cover are universal to all industries and situations.

It's been an incredible journey, and, in the process, I've learnt invaluable lessons in life and leadership from just the sheer experience of establishing and growing businesses and leading people globally.

When I formally sit down for the first time with new clients, they have, at times, shared with me the huge emotion, frustration and sometimes anger about the demands placed on them. This has also included tears from both male and female business owners who are in real despair.

No one needs to tell you as a business owner that owning your own business is a serious challenge with a lot of leadership responsibility.

When most people start a new business, they don't understand what leadership really is and the importance and responsibility they have to grow leadership behaviours and duplicate them throughout the business, so that the business can move forward and the business owner can have the choice to step back and be replaced.

This book has been written to encourage more business owners to grow key leadership behaviours so that they have the choice to replace themselves in their business and live better lives. However, the principles apply to anyone with leadership responsibilities who is leading teams in any industry.

Can I say again, replacing yourself doesn't mean you're out of your business, but what it does mean is having a deliberate process in place where the business can operate and grow with or without you, if you choose.

It's a personal choice you can make, because you can. You can spend as much or as little time as you like on the business because you've raised up skilled leaders around you to share the responsibility of leading and running your business.

Some days, business is totally unpredictable and 100% brutal, especially when everything you own is on the line and you're at capacity. Having the responsibility to grow your business as the owner, to keep providing for your family and your loyal staff, results in having work/life balance issues.

Some of the common challenges business owners must address so they can not only grow their business, but eventually replace themselves in the business, are:

- *How do I achieve the vision for my business?*
- *How do I attract and keep high-performing staff, so they don't leave and go elsewhere?*
- *How do I improve the culture of my business?*
- *How do I improve my cash flow?*
- *How do I attract and keep good clients?*
- *How do I achieve a work/life balance?*
- *How do I get my people to embrace change to grow the business?*
- *How do I encourage and motivate my people during the tough times to maintain their belief in the vision for the business and in me as the business owner?*
- *How do I get my people to take ownership and treat the business like it is their own?*

Replacing yourself as the business owner will require a deliberate strategy to grow and duplicate effective leadership behaviours.

Sometimes you can feel like you're a long way away from where you thought you'd be when you started your own business. The work/life balance you envisaged as a business owner has not eventuated. You have less time than you had before, are more personally invested, and have more pressure, stress and anxiety as you try to get your team to follow you by taking ownership.

It's my hope that this book will stimulate and agitate you to grow your leadership effectiveness so that you do have more time and less stress, and a high-performance team around you who have taken ownership of your business.

Since 2003, my Leadership Dynamics process has reduced huge pressures – including marital, financial, staff, health and relationship problems – for my clients.

The business owner was "IN" and not "ON" the business, which meant the business owned the owner; not the other way around.

In this book I'll outline six key leadership strategies which will grow and build the critical behaviours you need as a business owner to:

1. Get ON your business and not continually get caught up IN your business.
2. Attract and retain high-performing team members who are completely invested and take complete ownership of their roles and responsibilities.
3. Attract and grow loyal relationships with clients and customers.
4. Grow leaders around you to lead4growth so that you can delegate responsibility, and so that the business doesn't rely solely on you as the owner.
5. Ultimately achieve the work/life balance you imagined for yourself and your family when you started your business, by replacing yourself.

I know it's possible as I've been leading people in my own businesses since 1988, and many of my business alliances and clients (businesses both large and small, and elite sporting coaches and teams) have effectively implemented the Leadership Dynamics process since 2003 to grow their business and culture and replace themselves in order to live the life they imagined when they first started the business.

I was a simple bloke from the backstreets of Campbelltown, born to immigrant parents from Palmers Green, North London, England who moved to Sydney, Australia in 1965 when I was two years old. I'm the first person in my family's history to have my own business.

The one thing that I inherited from my parents was the will to win. Dad was a champion boxer and county cricketer and my mum played international hockey. The lessons I learnt from them was to believe in yourself and to never quit. These held me in sound stead to grow my businesses, particularly when the tough times came.

The one vision that still drives me today is seeing my parents work for somebody else and never having the opportunity to experience freedom by being able to replace themselves in their professions. I've never forgotten this, and it has been a driving force in my life.

My 84-year-old father today has regrets of not having spent enough time with my sister and me due to the huge demands and time pressures of his life as an electronics engineer. My father is a wonderful role model and a humble man for whom I have tremendous respect and who should have no regrets, doing the very best he could for his family.

I've always been inspired by the people in my life who've been able to replace themselves in their role or in their business to have a certain level of balance and choice in their life, experiencing real freedom, and that's what I want for you.

My Mission Statement for Leadership Dynamics is "To build stronger leaders to live better lives", by replacing themselves in the business. I've been doing this for myself since 1988 and for my clients since 2003, and what I treasure most is the deep, loyal, trusting and long-term relationships that have eventuated from this.

I know this book will stimulate and agitate your thinking and give you some practical strategies with which to grow your business so you can ultimately replace yourself, if you choose, allowing you the freedom owning your own business should bring.

Take care,
Peter

"Challenging. Passionate. Energising. Charismatic. Captivating. Galvanising. Leader. I don't use these words to describe Peter lightly. In fact, the impact that Peter has had on my thinking, my career, my leadership style, my decision-making and my influence are enormous. Peter has dedicated his life to understanding both the art and the science of leadership. He has sought leadership from business mentors for over 30 years and this has resulted in his incredibly unique perspective on how to grow your influence, build your teams and replace yourself."

— Damien Kelly,
Sales Director/Head of PHI, Aon, Australia

"We implemented the Leadership Dynamics process at a family Board level which resulted in us being "ON" our business formalising strategies and communication to grow the business, unifying the family. It has really challenged my thinking as a CEO about what true leadership is."

— Helen Gregory, Joint CEO, Gregory Jewellers

CHAPTER 1

Having been in business for myself since 1988, if there's one significant strategy that's resulted in some of the success I've experienced in my life and allowed me to replace myself in my businesses, it's **The Association Factor**.

The Principle of Association is central to human experience.

You can't escape the incredibly powerful Principle of Association if you truly want to be successful, as iron sharpens iron. You must always associate with people more successful and wiser than yourself and learn from them. Soak up what they know. They'll push you further than you'll ever push yourself – period. You'll not replace yourself in your business anytime soon unless you do.

However, I want to take the Principle of Association one step further and say that you not only need to *associate* with people more successful than yourself, but, as my mentor, Jim, taught me a long time ago, *you need to allow yourself to be led by someone who is more successful and wiser than yourself.* You need to be mentored by them, challenged by them, guided by them, called out by them, encouraged by them and empowered by them.

When I ask business owners who reach out to me, wanting to be mentored and grow their leadership, "Who leads you?", the answer nine times out of ten is, "I lead myself". I then ask, "How's that going for you?" and the common answer is, "That's why you're here, Coxey".

Owning a business is tough and it can be lonely, and at times you'll feel isolated. You'll never build anything great on your own – that's my business experience. Being led – which I still am today in my own life – is the number one strategy that begins the process of replacing yourself in your business.

Being led and being mentored taught me how to replace myself in my businesses through duplicating the key behaviours and strategies of the successful mentors who led me. Being led was the absolute game changer for me in both my professional and personal lives. It's the number one strategy I tell anyone who asks how to be successful.

Who leads you?

If you truly want to replace yourself, the first step to take your leadership to the next level is to have someone else lead you, and the more independent they are, the more effective this process will be.

In 1992, I had the good fortune to align myself with Jim, a very effective global entrepreneur, who led me for 22 years until his sad passing in August 2013.

It was the most significant implementation of a leadership strategy into my personal and business lives that without doubt, influenced my thinking and my behaviours when it came to leadership, contributing to the majority of success I've achieved in my life since 1992.

Being led independently developed my leadership potential and grew me as a leader.

All my clients who I have the leadership responsibility to lead as an independent leadership consultant will all highlight the tremendous value of being led by someone who is independent. They are leading-4growth with this deliberate leadership behaviour that they commit themselves to, to bring about effective change.

"Allowing myself to be led has increased my turnover by at least 15% and our profit margin is now up to 30%. Where before I would have scored a 4/10 on general, I would say I would now score an 8."

— Brent Lambert, CEO, PMC

"Allowing yourself to be led. That is probably the one at the top of the list because unless you are open to being led, the cumulative effect to create immediate necessary change will not occur."

— Francis Farmakidis, Partner, Vobis

There needs to be deliberate strategies and behaviours to develop people to lead. Being led independently is one of those strategies.

Author Michael Prichard stated:

"Fear is the darkroom where negatives are developed".

Let go of the fear and allow yourself to be led.

I want you to know the importance of being led for yourself, and to appreciate the great scope that it brings to those who truly commit to the process.

Leadership comes from inside you.

It's a spirit.

It's an attitude to always wanting to grow yourself as a leader and to grow the people you have around you, and a desire to want to grow personal accountability by being led.

Who is leading you?

Are you leadable?

Will you allow yourself to be led?

Who do you lead?

Why should someone follow you if you're not led by somebody else?

History is full of examples of great leaders being led:

The American mining mogul, Robert Friedland, led Steve Jobs.

Dr Ed Roberts, who invented the first inexpensive general-purpose computer, led Bill Gates. Bill also went to the American business magnate, Warren Buffett, for advice on numerous issues.

Don Graham, the CEO and Chairman of Graham Holdings, mentors Mark Zuckerberg.

Steve Jobs mentored Marc Benioff, an American internet entrepreneur, author and philanthropist, and founder of Salesforce.com.

Mahatma Gandhi mentored Dr Martin Luther King and Nelson Mandela.

Socrates led Plato.

Oprah Winfrey was mentored by celebrated author and poet, the late Maya Angelou.

Virgin Group co-founder Richard Branson asked British airline entrepreneur, Sir Freddie Laker, for guidance during his struggle to get multinational conglomerate Virgin Atlantic off the ground.

These leaders knew the value of being mentored by someone more experienced than themselves who was independent from their organisation and their vision.

They knew that if they didn't have the right thinking, behaviours and attitudes and if they weren't growing and improving, how could they expect their teams, or in some cases, nations, to grow?

These great leaders knew the value of allowing themselves to be led by someone:

- Who was independent.
- Who they could trust.

- Who brought greater wisdom.
- Who was not emotionally tied to them, their vision or the leaders they had around them.

Fresh eyes are a very powerful leadership strategy.

Throughout history, all the great leaders have been led – mentored by someone more successful than themselves – as they know it's the most effective way to bring about change.

If you research any successful person, without a doubt, you'll find that they've got a mentor and seek advice from others who are more experienced than themselves but, and most importantly, they know that their quality and effectiveness as a leader will be determined by their level of *teachability.*

Who is leading you?

Are you really listening?

Are you teachable?

Allowing yourself to be led by someone who is independent, who you can trust, and who aligns to your vision will lead to:

- Stimulation and agitation of your thinking.
- Enablement and empowerment, as it will give you greater self-confidence due to the belief your mentor has in you and the belief that will grow in yourself as a result of the process.
- Dedication. You're now accountable and that'll drive your commitment to leadership change.
- Validation about what your strengths are, which gives you clarity and empowers you.
- Maximising your leadership potential and the people you have around you.

If you really want to lead4growth, you need to demonstrate your ability to be inspired and be led by somebody else other than yourself who will challenge you.

- You need someone who challenges your status quo.
- You need someone who challenges your attitude.
- You need someone who challenges your spirit.
- You need someone who challenges your vision.
- You need someone who challenges your strategies.
- You need someone who challenges your team and environment.
- You need someone who challenges your relationships.
- You need someone who challenges your communication.
- You need someone who challenges your flexibility.
- You need someone who challenges your adaptability.
- You need someone who challenges your ego.
- You need someone who challenges your humility.
- You need someone who challenges your teachability.
- You need someone who challenges your ability to deal with conflict.
- You need someone to ask you: What leadership behaviours do you need to focus on that will lead to the results you want to achieve?

And all this, my friends, will lead you to being able to replace yourself in your business.

Are you prepared to be challenged and led in these areas?

It's not easy being challenged, but all the really significant and substantial accomplishments require those who wish to achieve them to be pushed well past their comfort zone.

If you want to bring about change, you as the leader must be truly willing to be part of the change process and to get uncomfortable.

You need to know where you must change. Often, we're so close to our business and our lives that we can't clearly see the changes that are so glaringly obvious to others who know better because they've walked the same road before us.

Leaders face the truth head on and are prepared to ask and tackle the difficult questions to enable them to lead more effectively.

Most people don't want to hear the truth and therefore never reach their leadership potential.

Do you want to reach your leadership potential?

Will you allow yourself to be challenged in areas that are going to stimulate and agitate you so that you will bring about change and allow you to replace yourself in your business?

Twelve months from now, if you change nothing and you are the same leader you are right now, with the same thinking and the same leadership issues, you'll still be where you are today.

Is that okay with you?

Here are six questions you truly and honestly need to ask yourself if you seriously want to replace yourself:

1. Are you really willing to be inspired?
2. Are you really prepared to change the way you think?
3. Do you really have a hunger to want to grow yourself as a leader?
4. Are you prepared to be challenged?
5. Are you willing to surrender to leadership sometimes that is not your own?
6. Will you allow ideas other than your own to help you lead better to lead4growth?

It takes a lot of humility, trust and respect to be led, but it's a key leadership strategy to grow your thinking and behaviours to lead4growth.

When people are led by an authentic leader who has a high level of influence, and meets with them regularly, this results in a much deeper level of empowerment of that individual. This in turn provides a very positive feeling and connection between the one who is leading and the one who is being led. Over time, as the level of trust and connection grows, the process of being led becomes increasingly effective in helping that individual grow and become more effective in their leadership.

As the leader, if something isn't going in the direction you need it to go, or you're not at the level of leadership you know you need to be at, or you haven't achieved the success in your business or personal life that you'd like to achieve, then allowing yourself to be led by someone who is independent to your business is a highly effective leadership strategy to get you to where you want to go. They'll ask the difficult questions that will result in a change in direction for you to lead4growth and ultimately replace yourself in your business, and allowing yourself to be led obviously has benefits for many areas of your life.

It's only when you're uncomfortable that leadership development occurs.

Are you uncomfortable?

What are you uncomfortable about?

If you're not uncomfortable, you're not pushing hard enough!

Are you prepared to feel uncomfortable in being led?

When was the last time you felt uncomfortable about change?

Who is challenging you?

Who is pushing you?

Are you prepared to face the truth head on and tackle the difficult questions to take your leadership to the next level?

How will your thinking change if you don't have anyone leading you?

Most people don't allow themselves to be led, and therefore, most people don't change the way they think, and they end up with the same results, day in, day out; week in, week out; year in, year out.

Rhythm is key!

A very important factor to the success of being led is that you must establish a disciplined and formal monthly rhythm to build trust and accountability. Being led builds momentum because of the implementation of change. Being led creates an emotional connection that builds over time with each meeting. The emotional connection leads to greater performance, which leads to greater trust, which leads to even greater performance.

As you continue to be led and you grow in your leadership, your level of influence in your team will increase and your confidence in your leadership skills will also grow – this is very empowering and raises your self-worth.

This result strengthens the trust and the relationship between you and the one who is leading you.

As trust increases, you open yourself up to the process in greater depth, allowing yourself to be challenged and pushed further. This process keeps repeating itself over the lifetime of the relationship – mine was for 22 years until Jim's sad passing; however, I now have another independent person who leads me.

When you allow yourself to be led, you are "ON" your business, "ON" your vision and "ON" your life, not caught up in them. It's the foundation upon which to grow and develop all the strategies I'm outlining in this book to help you replace yourself in the business and give you the freedom and lifestyle owning your own business should bring.

All my Leadership Dynamics clients, from the newest client to clients that I have been leading since 2003, understand the power and the effectiveness of being led independently. This strategy which they implement and execute in their lives, their people's lives and in their businesses, leads them for growth and they are all growing exponentially as they continue to develop their personal leadership potential and the leadership potential of the people they surround themselves with.

Are you "ON" your business or is your business "ON" you, owning you, and pushing you down?

If you're not being led by anyone, can I encourage you, as you finish this first chapter, to start thinking about who you could approach to do so? Think deeply about those you know who you'd like to be led by and make a short list, and then start asking from the top down.

My Leadership Dynamics process is a powerful way for business owners to get "ON" their business and "ON" their life, to replace themselves in the business.

Remember, all great leaders throughout history have allowed themselves to be led and all the leaders who will have an impact on our future world will also seek wisdom from those wiser than themselves.

Lord Chesterfield put it best:

"In seeking wisdom, thou art wise; in imagining that thou hast attained it, thou art a fool".

"Peter's Leadership Dynamics process has challenged our recruitment and retention processes when it comes to identifying

'natural' and 'emerging' leaders within our business and outside of our business.

Being challenged to change our thinking by someone who has an independent leadership process brought effective communication at a family board level and also helped identify key roles and responsibilities within our organisational chart that required significant formality and alignment.

Peter brought high-level leadership thinking into our business; if you want to lead – first you have to allow yourself to be led. Peter's conviction about this behaviour grows leadership, and results in better leaders coming into your business ..."

— Robert Gregory, Head of HR, Gregory Jewellers

"Peter Cox is one of the best leadership speakers I have had the privilege of being involved with. His high levels of passion and integrity allow him to deliver quality information and teachings, whilst allowing the audience to see it is possible for them. Peter has the ability to challenge you to be the best you can be. Not many people are able to do this with credibility. I would highly recommend Peter to anyone looking to use him in their business or personal life."

— Paul Dunn, Business Development Director, 360 Degree Marketing Group

"I've had the pleasure of working with Peter Cox for the last seven or eight years in a number of capacities, primarily as a leadership coach and mental coach for myself and a number of other leaders within the club. He's been instrumental in the success we've had over the last few years, culminating in a couple of premierships in the NRL competition. He worked with us on a weekly basis, one on one with our leadership group to develop our leadership strategies and improve not only on our individual performance but also the overall *performance of our team. Coxey's been an instrumental part of our team, a piece of the puzzle; has helped us come together and done a lot of hard work and we are forever grateful for his dedication to the Sea Eagles and his dedication to us as individual players to really help us out and perform to our potential in one of the toughest team sports in the world. We are forever grateful to Peter for his support and I certainly use a number of the qualities, leadership bits and pieces that he's taught me over the years in all aspects of my life."*

— Jason King, former Co-Captain of Manly Warringah Sea Eagles NRL Team, current General Manager – Elite Competitions, National Rugby League

CHAPTER 2

Growing Your Influence

Influence is all about affecting a person's heart and spirit.
If you want to lead successfully and ultimately replace yourself in your business, you need to have real and positive influence.

In the Star Wars movie *The Clone Wars*, Obi-Wan Kenobi used the Force to change the mind of one of the seedy characters who approached him in a bar to stop bothering him and to go and turn his life around. He just spoke the words and the guy was on his way to a life transformation. So great was the Force in Obi-Wan, that he had great influence over people and objects.

I thought how great it would be to have influence like that, but I'm not Obi-Wan Kenobi. For me to have influence will be determined by the type of person I am and whether I'm doing enough to impact people's lives that they want to follow me because of what I've done for them.

A leadership title, a position or a job description doesn't make you a leader.

Influence does.

You can be the CEO of a large multinational, the ruler of the free world, or the owner of a local business, but without influence, you'll truly lead no one because no one will be following you. Unless people follow you *willingly* instead of just turning up for a pay cheque each week, your influence won't grow.

In my own businesses I lead, my number one goal as the business owner is to ensure that the loyal, totally committed and respectful staff that I employ continue to want to follow me. For this to happen, I need to grow my influence. As a business owner, it's easy to get people in your team to follow you when things are going well, but when the tough times come is when you truly need influence to encourage those people that are closest to you to want to stand beside you and follow you over that mountain.

As a business owner and leader, you must have the hunger to want to continually grow your influence. When you grow your influence, you'll grow your results.

I am humbled and grateful to have special people in my business that are committed to my vision. It amazes me that some have been with me for 29 years and I'm a very driven and passionate business owner with very high expectations.

I believe that my influence with my staff, as strong as my leadership style is, grows because of my heart and spirit and the way in which I live my values – the FLITU Principle.

The **FLITU Principle** is my values, and all those closest to me know this. I strongly endeavour to live my life by this and it's a foundational part of my Leadership Dynamics process:

Family is everything to me.
Loyalty is earnt.
Integrity means my word is my word.
Trust is earnt and given, and easily lost if not respected.
Unity creates success as you can't do anything great on your own.

These are the principles that drive my decisions and behaviours – they give me a base, a compass with which to navigate through the myriad of choices I'm presented with each day in life and in business.

What values do you stand for?

What values would your people say you stand for?

If there's one thing I want more of in my life, it's to have more influence, not more money. Influence will result in people wanting to follow you with their whole heart, committing themselves to you, which will ultimately result in a higher level of success.

Leading4growth is your ability as the leader to have as much influence as you can by implementing the right influence strategies and having an effective leadership process to grow your influence so that you can then use the influence you have to develop your leadership team. Your leadership team are the people you surround yourself with, and they play a major role in determining how successful you become as the leader and business owner.

As you raise up leaders around you, you can then begin to replace yourself in the business if you choose, but, at the very least, you'll be growing the potential and performance of your people and your business.

You cannot lead if you don't have influence.

The more influence you have, the stronger your influence will become. It's cyclical.

> *"Influence is a key characteristic of a leader, if not THE most important one!"*
>
> **— John Maxwell**

If you had to score yourself out of 10, with 10 being extremely influential, what would you rate yourself?

Are you able to influence the people you lead to follow your vision?

When I look at my Leadership Dynamics clients, the dramatic change from when they started implementing my leadership process into their business to now, is nothing short of astounding in many cases.

> *"From January 2015 until August 2016, Peter Cox from Leadership Dynamics mentored me with a dynamic leadership program, one on one and with the Matildas, growing my leadership potential.*
>
> *My understanding of what leadership really was changed my behaviours, dramatically growing my influence, resulting in me becoming the Australian Women's Football Team Captain for the 2015 World Cup and 2016 Olympic Games. Coxey empowered and grew me, building me into a stronger leader."*
>
> *— Lisa De Vanna, former Captain of the Australian Women's Football Team, player for Serie A team, Fiorentina*

Without influence, you'll turn around and look back and realise no one is following you. You can't do anything great on your own! Influence is everything if you want to replace yourself! If no one is following you, you will never replace yourself, so what are you doing to grow your influence?

My mentor of 22 years, Jim, drove the word influence into my life to grow my leadership effectiveness. The greater your influence, the greater ability you'll have to lead your team to come with you on the journey and take your business to where you want it to go.

There are key factors that all highly effective and influential leaders continually focus on to increase their influence and my Leadership Dynamics process homes in on and grows these.

Here are some of those factors:

Be Led

This is key to growing your influence. When you have someone independent to your business who has your back and is building you up and encouraging you, but is also calling you out and challenging your decisions, and holding you accountable to do what you say you'll do, your influence will grow with this process. When your key people see you being led by someone independent to grow your leadership, this grows your influence because it gives you the authority and authenticity to lead others. When your leadership grows, so does your influence and when your influence grows, so does your leadership.

Who leads you?

Is your influence growing?

Is your team truly following you?

Have Strong Self-Belief

For you to have influence, you must have a high level of self-belief, combined with humility. If you don't believe in yourself as the leader, then why would your team want to follow you? Doubt and insecurity breed nervousness and undermine your influence as a leader. Having self-confidence, backed up by success is very powerful and if coupled with humility, will grow your influence.

Do you truly believe in yourself?

Do you have humility?

Can your team see that you believe in yourself?

Can your team see that you believe in them?

Have Integrity

Your team won't follow you if they can't trust you. You must be a person of your word, and your words and your actions must align.

It's crucial that the people you lead, the people who are closest to you and the people you surround yourself with know you're a person of integrity. When this happens, your influence increases due to you growing trust and it will lead to you being replaced in the business.

Integrity is a key pillar of my Leadership Dynamics process and I live the "I" of FLITU every day.

No doubt you too have come across people who don't have integrity, but you can't control what other people do. All you can do is control what you do when it comes to the "I" in FLITU, which will grow your influence and move you towards replacing yourself.

You cannot grow your influence if you don't have true integrity and there are people in leadership and in business who cannot understand why people don't want to truly follow them and it's because people don't fully trust them that their word is their word.

When people trust you, it means they'll follow you. If you don't have trust you don't have influence. Trust is everything.

Is your word your word?

Are you trustworthy?

Do you have trust?

Do you have integrity?

Integrity gives you credibility. You cannot lead without integrity. If your team doubts what you say and doubts what you do – even just occasionally in the small things – your credibility and your leadership will be undermined. To lead effectively, you always need to be a person of your word and walk the talk – you need to be credible, so you build the level of trust your team has in you.

What do you need to have more credibility about?

Having integrity drives your team to achieve great things, to push the boundaries. When your team believes in you, in your vision and in your genuine care of them, it makes them want to achieve and go further than ever before. Honesty and integrity feel like a lovely rarity these days, so for people to find it is like gold and it's inspiring!

Jim, my mentor, once casually recounted an incident during a trip to the Caribbean where he'd purchased a valuable piece of jewellery. Although he could have worn the jewellery through customs and claimed it as a personal possession, he declared its purchase, paid the duty on it and kept his conscience clean. Even in small, private situations away from the limelight of the board room, he showed integrity. This has had a profound impact on me to this day, and this and many other examples of his integrity led to my absolute loyalty to him as a leader as I trusted him completely. He grew our team and took us to new heights we could never have imagined for ourselves.

Add Value to the Lives of Those Around You

One of the most powerful ways you lead and grow your influence is by what you do for others – they want to follow you because of what you've done for them. People want to follow you because they see value in what you're doing for them. They recognise your skills, abilities, successes and people skills as a leader and they gladly follow, as they know they can trust you to grow them personally and professionally. You're the real deal – an authentic leader. Your influence increases when the people you lead know that you add value to their lives and that you truly care about them.

How do you show people you genuinely care for them?

What do you need to do to add more value to the lives of the people you lead?

Have Discipline and Self-Control

Influential leaders have the discipline to carry out the behaviours that lead to effective outcomes and to not do the things that distract them from achieving their vision. They stay focussed.

Just because you're busy, doesn't mean you're being effective for the long term.

When your people observe you focussing on the long term, being "ON" your business, this builds their confidence in you and grows your influence, which makes them want to follow you.

Business owners that are always caught up "IN" the business and not "ON" the business dilute their influence because they're not replacing themselves as the owner, which means the business is too reliant on them.

At times, when a new client contacts me and wants to implement the Leadership Dynamics process into their organisational structure, they reach out because they realise they're caught up "IN" and not "ON" the business, resulting in serious time management and work/life balance issues.

After many years of stress, they have an epiphany that they want a better quality of life, instead of just making a lot of money (which some of them already are), and that something seriously needs to change in what they're doing. As the business owner, if you're always in your business, you dilute your influence. The Leadership Dynamics process equips business owners in a big way to grow their influence.

Are you "IN" your business or are you "ON" your business?

Do you have a process to deliberately grow your influence?

Who's following you?

Who's not following you?

Are you focussed on the behaviours that will grow your long-term success?

Exercise Regularly and Eat Well

The Leadership Dynamics process is built upon the three-pronged holistic view I have of leadership:

1. Growing strong leadership thinking
2. Having a happy and balanced home life
3. Health and fitness

You cannot truly lead effectively and grow your influence if you don't have the right leadership thinking, the right home life and the right health. Everything you do will duplicate, good or bad, in all areas of your life. You must make the decision to lead by example in these three areas and it will grow your influence.

Having had my own businesses since 1988, I've seen business owners not replace themselves due to one of the above holistic leadership prongs being flawed.

Do you have the right leadership thinking?

Do you have the right home life?

Do you have the right health?

These are some of the many deliberate strategies that are part of my Leadership Dynamics process that I use to grow influence to build a loyal and committed leadership team around you, who take ownership of the business like it was their own, allowing you to replace yourself in the business.

"Over the months of working with Peter, I could just feel the strength and confidence building. He also pushed me really hard into this influence space. I think he knew quite well at the time that I didn't have it. There was a void there and the biggest void was my lack of influence. Today, I am just far more aware. I am aware of how I'm managing relationships and making decisions. My control is a lot better. I don't have the anxiety I used to have. I don't sweat the small stuff. There is a resilience of being confident; being positive, not losing your cool and not letting your empathy go."

— Kirsty Hunter, Managing Director,
EDIS Insights Pty Ltd

"The influence that I learned from Peter definitely helped me move from Sales Director to Managing Director. It has motivated me to firstly start looking at the bigger picture. I was a salesperson at heart and can sell very well and you always want to stay in your comfort zone. Working with Peter has opened my eyes to a lot of possibilities and ways of stepping back. Being in sales meant that I'm involved in the nitty gritty of every little thing and you can't look at the big picture – he's definitely helped me with the bigger picture and seeing the potential in it."

— Sam Vakili, Managing Director, MCR

"Peter has had a great influence on my life as a business leader. He came into my life in 2004 when, as a young entrepreneur, I recognised the need for assistance in my own leadership journey … I essentially needed someone to lead me.

He taught me that the number one responsibility of a leader is influence and as such nothing else matters…without influence nothing can be achieved."

—Simon Mair, Director, Laveer Partners

CHAPTER 3

H ere's my version of a true story to set the scene for this chapter…
The girl ran her trembling hands over her pant legs, smoothing non-existent wrinkles in an attempt to calm her heightening nerves that were threatening to squeeze the air from her lungs. It had taken a great deal of petitioning to be granted an audience with Charles VII, the Dauphin, heir to the French throne and now, she had to convince him that she was the one to lead his army to victory against the English.

Henry VI's men had captured a great deal of northern France and currently lay siege to the town of Orleans, a town of strategic importance for France's fate.

The girl told Charles that she'd had a vision in which God told her to lead the French army and reclaim Orleans.

A pretty bold claim for a girl of only 16 years.

She also made the prediction that there'd be a military reversal at the Battle of Rouvray, near Orleans.

Her prediction came true a few days later.

Needless to say, she made quite an impression on Charles and her urgent request to travel with the army and be given armour and weapons was granted.

Despite giving this girl leadership of his army, he did what a good Dauphin should do, and conducted a thorough background check. Upon her arrival, the young girl was quickly turning the battle into a religious war, so her authenticity and integrity had to be proven beyond a doubt. To cut a long story short, it was, and the girl was instrumental in the recapture of Orleans, garnering her further support and loyalty within the ranks of French government, the army and the church. Not bad for a 16-year-old farm girl!

The French, under this girl's leadership, went on to win many successive battles, claiming back much land, including the town of Reims, a town deep in the heart of English-occupied territory. When they took this town, the girl convinced Charles to be finally crowned as king. And on July 17, 1429, Charles VII's coronation took place. On December 29 of that year, the girl and her family were ennobled by Charles VII as a reward for all her actions.

In the words of Stephen Richey:

"She turned what had been a dry dynastic squabble that left the common people unmoved, except for their own suffering, into a passionately popular war of national liberation".

Unfortunately, a few months later in an ensuing battle, the girl was pulled off her horse by an archer and was captured. After a grossly unfair trial conducted by the English, she was sentenced to death and shortly thereafter, she was burnt alive at the stake …

This girl, known throughout history as Joan of Arc, was posthumously exonerated of all charges in a retrial, and remains forever in the hearts of the French and people around the world. [1,2] Her achievements leave most of us just shaking our heads in amazement and a little disbelief! She was an incredible leader from whom we can learn much.

Great leaders inspire us to achieve things we previously thought we couldn't achieve or didn't even see as an option. They take us into new territory, pushing us out of our comfort zones. Joan was an incredible source of inspiration for her people – she led them to totally commit to the vision to regain their freedom from the British and do whatever it took to achieve it, including trusting a 16-year-old girl to lead an army.

She was never swayed from her task by the initial disbelief of many – she kept true to the vision God had given her and inspired thousands to rally to her banner and do whatever it took to win.

> *"History shows us that the people who end up changing the world – the great political, social, scientific, technological, artistic, even sports revolutionaries – are always nuts, until they are right, and then they are geniuses."*
>
> **— John Eliot (Personal Excellence.co)**

The thing that was fundamental to Joan's success (besides having the backing of God), was having a crystal-clear vision. It drove every behaviour and captivated every thought and she cast that vision SO clearly to those around her, to her army and to her nation.

A critical component to your success, is for you to have a crystal-clear vision of where you want to go and what you want to achieve, so you can ultimately replace yourself in your business sooner rather than later.

Your vision should be driving every decision you and your people make – it's the beacon of hope, the end goal upon which everyone and everything is focussed and striving for.

Without a clear vision, you and your team are like a rudderless ship in stormy seas, being pushed around by other people's decisions and actions because you're unsure of where you're actually headed, so you're swayed by what sounds good at the time, though in reality, you'd rethink those decisions if you had a clear vision of where you actually wanted to go.

What's your vision for your business?

Do you want to take your business somewhere you haven't been before?

Do you know how you're going to make your vision become a reality?

Is your vision realistic?

For you as the business owner to accomplish your vision, whether it's breaking new ground and pioneering new frontiers, or becoming the best in your industry, for example, there are a number of critical strategies which all work together, each component relying on the other, to drive the results you want to achieve. If you don't lead and implement all these vision strategies, it'll impact other areas of your business and will jeopardize your chance of achieving your vision and replacing yourself. Here are several of those key strategies.

Formalise Your Vision

Firstly, as the business owner, you need to write your vision down in a formal document, at the very least – having it in your head won't cut it. Writing it down helps you and your people to become crystal clear on exactly what your vision is. Put your vision on the office wall for the entire team to see and include your vision at the end of all your emails, and on all key company documents, for example.

Formalising your vision will grow accountability and ownership and is a must-do leadership step! Accountability and ownership are vital. When you grow accountability, you grow ownership and you can only do this through *formality*.

If you're being led by a mentor, explain your vision to them so they can hold you accountable for achieving it. Don't be afraid of accountability – embrace it – all great and aspiring leaders do! Accountability drives success.

Have you formalised your vision? If so, how?

If not, how could you?

Who are you accountable to, to achieve your vision?

Communicate Your Vision

You can't do anything great on your own and, if you want to replace yourself in your business, you need the people you surround yourself with to know where you want the business to go, and for them to treat the business like it was their own.

The only way your key people will know and understand your vision is if you communicate it effectively with formality and empower them with it to make them want to follow you, completely committing to your vision.

Formalising your vision into a powerful visual presentation and formal document, and delegating responsibility to your key people, grows accountability and ownership.

A vision creates power, which results in positive energy within your team. A great leader has the ability to communicate the vision and cause the team to embrace and own it.

Does the team really understand the vision?

Does the team really believe in the vision?

Is the team personalising the vision?

Can the team communicate the vision?

Is the team truly committed to the vision?

Your vision provides meaning for you and your team to get out of bed in the morning and fight for it, because achieving a vision is not easy.

You either have hope or hopelessness and when you effectively cast your vision, the team believes.

Does your team have hope?

Does your team believe?

Does your team have energy?

Do you?

Thomas Watson Junior, CEO of his father's office machine company, was so overwhelmed by his sense that computers would be everywhere, even when they were nowhere, that he placed the company on the line and advocated for his vision of a future society driven by computers and the part the company should play in it. The company: IBM. In 15 years, Thomas Watson Junior grew IBM from a revenue of $892 million and 72,000 employees, to a revenue of over $8 billion and more than 270,000 employees, transforming the company into one of the largest corporations in the world. Among many accomplishments, IBM was instrumental in the development of the computer. Thomas's character and convictions formed a powerful impression on thousands of IBM employees around the world – from the board room to the branch office – and even on people who joined the company long after he had left it. [3,4]

A vision is not fancy words in a gilded frame hanging in the foyer – it's down in the trenches; it's a lived-out reality that starts from the top down, with everyone knowing and owning the vision, just like Thomas Watson Junior and Joan of Arc.

Be Passionate!

No great vision is ever achieved without fire in the belly.

Michael Jordan, the world's greatest basketballer once said:

"I realised that if I was going to achieve anything in life I had to be passionate.

I had to get out there and go for it. I don't believe you can achieve anything by being passive. I know fear is an obstacle for some people, but it is an illusion for me".

Passion is when you put more energy into something than is required. It's more than just enthusiasm or excitement; passion is ambition that has materialised into action – it's when you put as much heart, mind, body and soul into something as is humanly possible.

Does your vision create emotion within you and your team?

Does the vision stir the hearts and spirits of you and the people you lead?

Are you passionate about your vision?

Is your team passionate about your vision?

Keep Focussed on the Future and Stay Positive

Another factor in casting vision for your business and your people is that you as the business owner must always remain optimistic, focussed on the future and on seeing what's possible, no matter what's going on, including a battle literally raging around you, like Joan of Arc, or when you've experienced a major setback to achieving the vision. Your team is relying on you to lead them through and show them the way forward. If you don't have faith, why should they? And if your team doesn't, you won't be able to replace yourself in the business.

Are you focussed on the future?

Are your people focussed on the future?

All effective leaders communicate and live their vision day in, day out – it's so much a part of them that they can't help it. They keep bringing themselves and their people back to the vision with everything they do, ensuring that their people's thoughts and actions are aligned to it.

What must you do to live your vision, day in, day out?

Are you bringing your team back to your vision?

What do you need to be more inspirational about?

A point that's important to note here, when thinking about your vision and about the future, is to be tempted to believe that our past will play out in the future – that it will form the foundation for it. Sometimes it will, but sometimes it won't – good or bad.

Are you really focussed on the future?

Are you trusting your past to be your future (good or bad) without proper analysis?

Create Momentum

Casting vision and focussing on the future is essential for you to create and maintain momentum for achieving your vision and replacing yourself. Without momentum, you won't progress. Your business will stagnate and, worse, go backwards. You need a deliberate leadership process to grow and maintain momentum.

Just because you have momentum today doesn't mean you'll have momentum tomorrow – momentum is fragile and precious and requires effective and optimistic leadership.

If you're feeling stuck, here are some thoughts for you to take hold of to get you moving and create momentum for yourself and your people:

- Age has nothing to do with stepping out of your comfort zone.
- Keep moving, keep changing, keep growing.
- Your thinking must be bigger, so that you have the ability to open yourself up to something new that you've never done before.
- Sometimes you follow in someone else's footsteps, before you create your own steps (being led).
- There will come a time when you create your own steps.
- The miracle happens in the first step.
- Make a decision and never look back.
- When you move by taking a step forward, you'll become unstuck and will begin to create momentum, one step at a time.

What must you do to create more momentum in your team?

What would be your first step?

Don't Get Distracted

You need extreme focus to achieve the vision and replace yourself. You mustn't let yourself get distracted from the things you need to accomplish to achieve it. Don't let others dictate your actions – make your plans with your team and keep each other accountable for achieving them.

Plan each day ensuring you're focussing on the things that will help achieve the vision, and don't deviate from it. Increase your focus and you'll increase your growth.

What needs greater focus right now?

What's distracting you?

Are you focussed on the right things to achieve your vision and replace yourself?

I know this chapter has given you some insight into the importance of casting vision for your business. You've seen how it becomes the rudder for you and your people to navigate your way through the stormy seas of life and business, to end up where you want to go and help you replace yourself in the business, if and when you so choose.

There are many things that go into not only casting vision but also achieving it and I trust the number of key leadership strategies that I've touched on in this chapter will stimulate and agitate you to cast your vision with greater effectiveness.

My Leadership Dynamics process provides business owners like yourself with a structure and proven strategies to effectively implement their vision into their business and lead it to fruition, as my many clients will attest to.

"We've been working with Coxey for a six-month period and whilst it's only been a short amount of time, we've had some notable achievements. By investing wholeheartedly in Peter's Leadership Dynamics process, my business partner and I have achieved some great results for our business. In our time together, Peter has helped us get 'unstuck' in our personal and business life. He has shown us that on-going belief and a change in daily behaviours, contribute to bringing us closer to our end game. He's taught us how to create unbreakable focus despite all of life's distractions and ingrained within us how to focus on 'behaviours that drive results, rather than focus on only the results' – a complete opposite approach to many of the business coaches/ experts we have worked with in the past.

As a result, some of the things that we have achieved together include: winning a prestigious design award as the 'Best Brand Agency' in Sydney, an award that we would never have applied for; increasing our following across all social media channels by an average of 21%; a shift in daily sales activities have increased our new business pipeline by 26%; and the increase in our own brand awareness has led to over a dozen articles as a branding expert published in mainstream media. This has now extended to invitations to speak at various events and expos as an industry authority alongside other high-profile brands.

And these results have been achieved in working with Peter for only six months – we are very excited about our future.

We would recommend anyone who is thinking about working with Leadership Dynamics who want to lead for growth, to start out by spending five minutes with Peter … your business (and life) will never be the same.

— Stella Gianotto, Branding Expert and Creative Director, Brand for Brands Agency

Sources:

1. www.history.com/topics/middle-ages/saint-joan-of-arc
2. www.nationalgeographic.com/archaeology-and-history/magazine/2017/03-04/joan-of-arc-warrior-heretic-saint-martyr/
3. www.ibm.com/ibm/history/exhibits/chairmen/chairmen_4.html
4. www.ibm.com/ibm/history/exhibits/watsonjr/watsonjr_intro.html

CHAPTER 4

Setting Clear Expectations

Actor Ryan Reynolds once said:

"When you have expectations, you're setting yourself up for disappointment". [1]

Have you had high hopes and then been let down, in the past?

Whatever your history may be, and whether or not this statement by Mr Reynolds has some merit, I'd like to counter it by saying:

Without clear expectations you are setting yourself up for FAILURE!

If you as the business owner don't have expectations of yourself and the team you lead, you're heading nowhere, wasting everyone's time, and you certainly won't be able to replace yourself in the business.

In Chapter 3, I talked about the importance of casting vision for your business – the importance of formalising it, making yourself and your team accountable to it, and the need to ensure you effectively communicate your vision to your team so that you inspire them to own it. It's vital the team feels part of it and that they know the important role they have in the big picture, as you can't achieve your vision on your own!

If your team doesn't own the vision, you'll be a long way from replacing yourself in the business!

Setting clear expectations for your team is vital for your team to not only take ownership of the vision but to ensure they know what to do to achieve it.

A recent workplace poll of companies around the world by Gallup [2] found that only about half of employees strongly agree that they know what's expected of them at work, and that knowing what's expected of them is a major driving factor of employee engagement, which, according to Gallup, is around only 13% worldwide! A sobering fact.

This makes it incredibly hard for employees to meet let alone succeed at performance goals if they don't know what they are, and they're not engaged! Even if you have motivated employees who want to work hard, if they don't know what you really want them to work on, they focus on things counter-productive to your vision. And this in turn makes it very difficult for you to achieve what you want to achieve with the business, and eventually replace yourself. For example, your people might know the overall vision of the company is to expand into Asia by 2021, but what does it mean for them? How does it translate into everyday activities? What will determine their contribution to the business to achieve this?

Not having clear performance expectations is like trying to find your way to the bathroom in a friend's house in the middle of the night – groping and feeling your way through unfamiliar territory, hoping you'll make it to the end goal without stumbling over or crashing into too many things along the way.

William Wallace was a legendary thirteenth-century Scottish freedom fighter who was made even more famous through his depiction in Mel Gibson's movie, *Braveheart*. In the scene of the Battle of Stirling Bridge, we see a vastly outnumbered Scottish army – the Scottish troops are assembled in the rolling, early morning mist, nervously calculating the odds of success and survival; should they run and live, or stay to fight and probably die? The English troops present an imposing and impressive foe. Some of the Scottish troops start to turn and flee and it's about then that William Wallace gives his impassioned speech:

"Yes. Fight and you may die. Run and you will live, at least awhile. And dying in your bed many years from now, would you be willing to trade all the days from this day to that, for one chance to come back here as young men, and tell our enemies that they may take our lives, but they will never take our freedom?"

William and his commanders then harnessed the loyalty and passion the speech evoked with a clever and well communicated military plan – each division clearly knowing their part to play in crushing the English army.

As the enemy progressed across the narrow Stirling Bridge, the Scots waited until half of them had passed and then they killed the English as quickly as they could cross. Then, when the English cavalry were sent, the Scots' schiltron formations forced the infantry back into the advancing cavalry. This charge, led by one of Wallace's captains caused some of the English soldiers to retreat as others pushed forward and, under the massive weight, the bridge collapsed and many English soldiers drowned, giving the Scots a significant victory.

The Scots, though at an apparent disadvantage, triumphed. Wallace emboldened the Scottish army with his vision for Scotland and then most importantly via his captains, clearly gave each man the role they needed to play to achieve victory.[3,4,5] He and his team gave their best and inspired the army to do the same with a clear vision and clear performance expectations. A powerful combination.

For you to lead4growth and replace yourself in your business, it'll only be possible when you develop and communicate clear expectations for each member of your team. It's like oxygen. Essential. And they can inspire legendary performances.

Have you set clear expectations for your people?

Do they know what their role is in helping to achieve the vision?

Do they know what you expect from them in their role?

Do they know what outcomes you want to achieve?

There are many key things you need to do when setting clear expectations to ensure individuals and the team achieve the vision. Having a process, like my Leadership Dynamics process, will ensure you set the right expectations to achieve the right results.

The following are a few of the key strategies that form part of my leadership process that you need to consider when setting clear expectations for your people.

Break Your Vision Down

Once you've established your vision, you need to break it down into a plan to achieve it. You need to set measurable long-term yearly and monthly targets and determine the strategies and tactics you need to implement to achieve them. This needs to be done for each division or department of your business and then for each person in them.

When developing goals for each individual team member's performance expectations, you must consider a number of factors, including:

1. The needs of the organisation
2. The needs of the team
3. The motivation of each individual
4. The skills of each individual
5. The different personalities of each individual in your business
6. Their position on the Emotional Guidance Scale (developed by Abrahams and Hicks)

If you don't, your performance goals will be poorly developed and will lead only to demotivate and frustrate your team.

To be successful, your performance goals must motivate and keep team members focussed on the big picture and this means ensuring you include the above-mentioned factors in setting your expectations for your people.

Have you taken into consideration the above when setting expectations of your people?

Do you know what the motivation, skills and personality types are of your key people?

Do you know where your people are on the Emotional Guidance Scale?

The Leadership Dynamics process is extremely effective at determining what the motivations, skills, and personality type are for each key individual in your team, and where they are emotionally.

Determine the Expected Thinking to Grow the Right and Expected Behaviours

Once you've established your vision and you've developed a plan of how you're going to get there, you also need to determine the *thinking and behaviours* that are required to achieve the vision.

These need to become the expected thinking and behaviours of yourself and the team you lead, and it's critical that they're clearly communicated so they result in the development of your business culture.

A winning team culture (which I'll cover in Chapter 5), is foundational to the success of your entire business and drives your expectations to achieve the vision, which will ultimately enable you to be replaced in the business (if you choose).

Have you determined the thinking and behaviours you expect of your team to achieve your vision?

Have you determined the key values of your culture that you need to succeed?

Are you leading by example?

Are you living your values and behaviours?

Clearly Communicate Your Expectations

Each team member must have a clear understanding of the performance expectations required, and the strategies and tactics they need to help achieve this. You can't simply email your team members the expectations you have, or mention them in a group meeting and expect your team to have a solid understanding of what you mean. You and your key leaders must communicate your expectations one on one with each team member, allowing for questions, discussion and feedback to ensure absolute clarity.

It's critical that you also set a formal time with each team member on a regular basis to track how they're doing in achieving their performance expectations to grow accountability. Accountability is key for your people achieving their performance expectations.

Do you have an effective process for not only developing you and your team, but also for communicating and keeping you and your people accountable for your expectations?

Do you have a process for evaluation?

Do you have an accountability process?

Do you have a communication strategy and process which provides clarity in relation to each team member's role and how they fit into the big picture?

While most of us will never literally command an army where each move results in the life or death of thousands, as leaders and business owners we do however have the immense responsibility to lead our teams to the best of our ability. Business owners must lead by example, to inspire those they lead with an awe-inspiring vision and then to empower team members to own it by establishing clear performance expectations they are held accountable for achieving.

Without this clarity, growing accountability and responsibility when poor performance occurs is more difficult and it will reduce the chances of a winning performance, and of you being able to replace yourself in the business. You must ensure that as the business owner, you implement a highly effective and proven leadership process to do this.

My Leadership Dynamics process is proven in creating and communicating clear expectations to individuals and teams and holding them accountable for achieving expectations that have been set.

"Setting clear expectations came from putting formality into our business. When we first met Peter that was the first thing he said to us. I think the thing that resonates with us is how much are you prepared to pay to love your life. It's a really clever thing he said and we often come back to that. Putting formality into our business was the catalyst. It encouraged us to develop a structure right throughout the business and led us down the path of corporatizing. The formality that was introduced to us by Peter and surrounding ourselves with the right people was the best thing that ever happened to us. It has developed right throughout our business."

*— **Tony Hargreaves and Andrew Melville,**
Managing Directors, Renascent*

"Peter's process broke down communication walls in our business that we didn't even realise existed, leading to a more open, collaborative and productive team. His process agitates and stimulates, empowering the leaders of InfoTrust to lead from the front with confidence."

— Dane Meah, CEO, InfoTrust

Sources:

1. www.brainyquote.com/quotes/ryan_reynolds_587226
2. Five Ways to Improve Employee Engagement Now. Gallup. www.gallup.com/workplace/231581/five-ways-improve-employee-engagement.aspx
3. www.history.co.uk/biographies/william-wallace
4. en.wikipedia.org/wiki/William_Wallace
5. www.stellarleadership.com/docs/Leadership/articles/Leadership%20and%20Braveheart%20Speech%20Transcript.pdf

CHAPTER 5

Building Team Culture

O ne of the biggest challenges for any business is to grow the right culture – a culture where people thrive and it drives them towards excellence, growing their leadership and resulting in high-performance teams.

Business owners must realise that to grow culture is relentless – you can never stop, and if you truly want to replace yourself you must have a deliberate process in place which drives the culture of your business without you.

In the business world I believe the major advantage you have over your competitors is the people you surround yourself with and the culture you build.

People and culture are your edge and will allow you to replace yourself in your business.

When a new client connects with me and I go into their business for the first time, within 60 minutes I will discern whether the culture is good or bad.

Culture is Leadership

If you can't grow your culture, then you won't grow your people and if you don't grow your people, you won't grow your business and you won't replace yourself in the business.

The number one asset in any business is the people.

To achieve a stellar performance from your team to achieve your vision, you need to build a winning team culture. You can't build anything great on your own so it's critical you build your culture. Without it, you will do nothing great and you certainly won't be in the position to replace yourself in the business.

Culture can be defined as the collective norms, rituals and behaviours that a group of people share – their way of life; their way of thinking and behaving, but as the anthropologist, Clifford Geertz, defines, it also includes symbols being transmitted through time within a system.

Since 1988, culture has meant everything to me. If you have great people in the wrong culture, you'll lose as they'll become demotivated, disengaged, under-utilised and will probably go elsewhere. However, I've seen time and time again that even if you have people with not as much talent, but you have an unbelievable culture in which they can grow, you start winning. And, the sky's the limit when you attract highly talented people to your business because of your culture.

A winning team culture is a powerful force. It sparks hope in the darkest of times, moving people forward regardless of what challenges they face; it instils in people a deep sense of belonging and a desire to want to belong to something greater than themselves. It motivates people to want to excel at what they do and push further, not ever satisfied with the level of their performance – there can always be a better way. Individuals in the team work as one organism, supporting and spurring one another on.

Your culture won't change overnight – it's something that requires your leadership, focus and commitment as the business owner, and that of each and every one of your people, for the long haul. You just need to start and your momentum will grow.

What's the culture like in your business?

Is it the culture you'd like to see?

How could you improve it?

My Leadership Dynamics process is highly effective at building and maintaining a winning team culture within the business, and it's been doing this effectively in all of my businesses since the late 1980s and in all my clients' businesses since 2003, when Leadership Dynamics was launched.

There are five key elements that I believe go into building and growing a winning team culture, that my Leadership Dynamics process focusses upon deliberately:

Each element depends on the other and has a key role in developing a winning team culture, which results in a high-performance team.

The picture of the upside-down pyramid with the heart and spirit at the top and then filtering down to trust, mental toughness and then physical (positive energy) will ultimately determine the effectiveness of your culture to grow and drive people to high performance without you, so you can be replaced in the business.

The Heart and Spirit

You must start with the heart and spirit of your people and Leadership Dynamics has a deliberate process to do this and I've implemented this process over 15,000 times. The number one asset of any business is its people. Nothing else. Not you. Not the products or services you provide, but your people. If you remember only one thing from this chapter, remember this:

The product is not the product. The product is people!

This should drive your leadership.

My Leadership Dynamics process is a systemised way to bring about a change in the hearts and spirits of people in your business, and I've effectively used it to help my clients to grow their business, some up to 1000%, focussing on these two areas of the heart and spirit of their people – focussing on growing them as individuals and growing their leadership potential.

When you have individuals who are strong on the inside, who are positive and whose thinking is in alignment with you and your vision, you have a solid foundation on which to build a winning team culture.

Do you consider your people your greatest asset?

Do you invest in your people as your number one asset?

What is the heart and spirit like of the people you lead?

"Very rarely do people come into your life that help steer you in another direction. For some people, it never happens. I was introduced to Peter through my father when I was in my mid-twenties. It was an introduction that I will forever be grateful for. I was looking to embark on my journey into business and meeting Pete and his wife Deb coincided perfectly with where I was at. Over the years, Pete has led me and taught me invaluable life lessons. The most valuable of which – people. Learning to understand and relate to people. Every major success I have had across my businesses, I can tie back to the principles that Pete taught me and the literature that he recommended. I can confidently say that I can now build rapport with anyone, thanks to Pete. Today, we're close friends, colleagues, business partners and family. I hope that one day you find your 'Coxey'. He or she is out there, you just need to find them. Enjoy the book and enjoy the journey."

*— **Matt Jones, Founder,***
*****Tradie Web Guys and TheSiteShed.com*****
*****Partner – Tradiematepro*****

Trust

Only when you get the heart and spirit right will you earn trust. If you have trust issues, you're developing a losing team culture, and no one will follow you as the owner and leader. Leadership is a responsibility and effective leaders earn and re-earn and grow trust. You won't achieve the results you want to achieve if you have trust issues in your team.

Do you have trust issues within the team you lead?

Who trusts you?

Who doesn't trust you?

Who don't you trust?

Achieving your vision for your business (and ultimately replacing yourself) means displaying a consistent and predictable character as the leader, day in, day out, in public and in private. That way, people will always know you can be trusted and that you're dependable. Remember, as the leader, your actions are always under close scrutiny.

"Look up, Harry ... you are no longer Colcord, you are Blondin. Until I clear this place, be a part of me, mind, body, and soul. If I sway, sway with me. Do not attempt to do any balancing yourself. If you do, we will both go to our death."

This is a quote from an incredible true story of trust that really impacted me and showed me exactly what trust is – it's the story of the life of French acrobat, Jean François Gravelet, who is better known in the history books as Charles Blondin. Charles Blondin was the first man to ever cross Niagara Falls on a tightrope. And he did so with no safety net or harness. By the end of his career, it was reported that he'd crossed Niagara Falls over 300 times! There were many instances where he carried a stove and cooking supplies to the middle of the tightrope and cooked an omelette which he then lowered down to the people below on the Niagara Falls tour boat, *The Maid of The Mist*. Sometimes, Charles liked to have a glass of champagne in the middle, or carry a camera on his back and take a photo of the swarming crowds of onlookers, or hang upside down on the wire, or walk backwards across the tightrope. But the time that he crossed the Falls that is a demonstration of true trust is the day that Charles's manager, Harry Colcord, crossed with him, clinging to his back! What faith and trust in Charles's ability! Charles had displayed his skills on the tightrope over the Falls time and time again, in a multitude of varying conditions, so Harry Colcord could look past his fear and trust Charles to get them safely across to the other side. What a thrilling ride, to say the least![1,2] This is the type of trust you need as a business owner from your people to build a winning team culture.

Would your people follow you across your "Niagara Falls" because of their complete trust in you as the leader?

Are they that in sync with you and you with them?

What trust issues do you need to resolve?

Where do you have trust?

Where don't you have trust?

I spend 75% of my time working on the heart and spirit of people with my Leadership Dynamics process. When you spend time with people, it's amazing what comes out of their heart and spirit. When I go into a new client's business, there are always underlying issues that must be dealt with head on so you can grow alignment and grow trust. As business owners, this can often mean making some tough decisions to resolve the issue, but if you don't, the problem festers and worsens, and your influence will be weakened as your people see you ignoring or procrastinating about the problem.

Are you willing to make the tough decisions to resolve issues within your business?

Are you procrastinating about an issue you need to resolve that affects the heart and spirit of your people?

"Peter has helped our business grow substantially by providing us with leadership skills and helping us make hard decisions that we would not have normally made."

— Pat Curran, Owner, Curran Plumbing

"What I have taken away so far from Leadership Dynamics is the ability and courage to make hard decisions which has allowed me to become a better leader."

— **Josh Eaton, COO, Starleaton**

Mental Toughness

Only when you get trust do you get mental toughness.

Mental toughness is positive thoughts under pressure.

It's very easy to think positively, when you're winning, when you're succeeding, when you have momentum.

The real key to building a winning team culture is to have your people thinking positive thoughts when they aren't winning, when they're under pressure, when they feel they're under the pump. And when you get positive thoughts under pressure, which is mental toughness, you will get positive and physical energy, not negative energy, in relation to what's going on in your culture.

Do the individuals in the team you lead have positive thoughts when they're under pressure?

Do you have positive energy or negative energy in the team you lead?

It's not easy to get people to think positively about themselves and about their teammates when they're not currently succeeding, when they're not winning and particularly if they believe many don't have confidence and faith in their ability. It can be incredibly demotivating and can strip the energy out of your people. I've witnessed incredibly talented individuals doubt themselves and their ability when their team isn't currently successful.

It takes a very deliberate leadership process to develop and maintain mental toughness and positive energy, and this is what my Leadership Dynamics process does.

Do you have a winning team culture?

Do you have an effective leadership process to not only grow but maintain a winning team culture?

Are you surrounded by a high-performance team?

Are you being replaced in your business?

Are people growing in your business?

You never stop building culture – culture is leadership, which means you never stop growing your leadership potential or the leadership potential of the people you surround yourself with. The Leadership Dynamics process is a deliberate process to do this and replace business owners in their business.

The moment you as the leader and the business owner take your culture for granted and you take your eyes off it, your culture will suffer and ultimately, so will your business. You can see some organisations today that were once at the very top, who are now a shadow of their former selves because of loss of leadership resulting in the loss of culture.

What are you doing to grow your culture?

"Peter's Leadership Dynamics process stimulated my thinking about what authentic leadership really is and what is required to evolve as a leader and evolve leadership within our family business. Peter's process will challenge the way you think to grow the necessary behaviours that lead to effective leadership. The formalised one on one process is a very effective tool to lead people and grow

leadership within an organisation by growing accountability and respect within the organisation's culture. If you want to grow your leadership potential, the leadership development process will stimulate and agitate you to do this ..."

— **Edward Gregory, Joint CEO, Gregory Jewellers**

Two Key Platforms That Build A Successful Business

There are two key platforms that build a successful business:

1. *Accountability:* a culture in which individuals, teams and the business are expected to achieve and meet all expectations that were agreed to, resulting in the results you want to achieve being achieved.
2. *Respect:* a culture in which people are empowered, cared for and valued.

The Leadership Dynamics process drives these two platforms with a formalised strategy.

When I go into teams and businesses, I either see accountability or I don't. I either see respect or I don't.

Do you have accountability?

Do you have respect?

If you don't have accountability and you don't have respect, you will never be replaced in your business.

I have a great deal of conviction about implementing deliberate strategies to grow accountability and respect within businesses and teams. Your ability to grow your business and replace yourself in the business will be determined by the level of accountability and respect you build.

If I were to ask you what the levels of accountability and respect existing within your business are, could you tell me?

You have to really be able to analyse and answer the question above because if you don't have accountability and you don't have respect, the results you want to achieve will not happen.

My Leadership Dynamics process is highly effective in not only determining the level of accountability and respect that you have within your business and *why* you have it, but also *growing* the level of accountability and respect through formalisation, strengthening your culture and growing the performance of your people into a high-performance team. Only when you have a high-performance team will you be able to have the choice to be replaced in your business.

The Three Key Elements of Accountability and Respect

There are three key elements of accountability and respect:

1. *Traits:* a distinguishing characteristic or quality
2. *Beliefs:* a state of mind, habits, behaviours and confidence
3. *Values:* a set of principles of right conduct

Accountability and respect each have certain traits, beliefs and values that my Leadership Dynamics process focusses on and grows within individuals and teams.

You never stop building and growing a winning team culture. It'll take total commitment and dedication from you as the leader and business owner to drive it; it's your responsibility to grow it and you must lead by example. All great and effective leaders build a winning team culture, as they know that without it, they will not achieve their vision and won't have any chance of replacing themselves.

Culture drives and underpins everything you do. If you have a winning team culture, you'll grow and you'll achieve your vision. If you don't have a winning team culture, you won't experience success.

> *"After a chance meeting with one of Peter's long-term clients, it was clear from the first presentation that what Leadership Dynamics had to offer our business was long overdue. Having spent the past five years going through a series of acquisitions, blending cultures was our number one challenge coupled with the complications of family business succession planning.*
>
> *Operating a business with ~70 staff across eight locations in two countries lends itself to many challenges of which many are overwhelmingly rewarding. Seeing the impact of investing in our people has without a doubt been my most rewarding strategic move in my six years as CEO. Not only is there a heightened level of performance, but the impact Peter and the Leadership Dynamics course has had on our team's personal lives was an unexpected benefit. Proving that in this day and age of everything being fast paced and on demand, it is possible to have a work/life balance that maximised productivity.*
>
> *Being intrusted to be the figurehead of our group, I had under-estimated the need to be engaged with my own formalised leadership coaching. The changes in my own behaviour with greater focus on unity, edification and empowerment have meant I have a much stronger leadership group working around me. I can see Peter being an integral part of our business strategy as we plan toward building future plans for the fourth generation of the Starleaton group."*
>
> — **Ben Eaton, CEO, Starleaton**

"I commenced my role in September 2014. Soon upon commencement I realised that one of the big areas lacking in the team environment was leadership and behavioural change. I sought the help of an expert and was quickly led to Peter Cox and his Leadership Dynamics process. We immediately formed a partnership and a relationship that lasted nine months up until we went to the FIFA World Cup in 2015 in Canada. Peter Cox added great value to our team in terms of leadership, in terms of identifying leaders, creating leaders and developing their skills within the field of leadership. He's a great asset to our team in terms of building all the skills that are required and certainly creating an environment that's challenging and stimulating for all the players and staff.

For me personally, he added great value – always challenging, always finding ideas on how to improve my own leadership. So, I couldn't recommend anyone more highly for a group, a business or an executive team other than Peter Cox and his Leadership Dynamics team. Great help to our team and certainly added great value to all players and staff along the process and I'm sure he'd be able to help you out in your business or your elite sporting team."

— *Alen Stajcic, former Head Coach,*
The Australian Women's Football Team

"When I meet with Peter, he keeps me honest, accountable and true to the vision; he has an intense personality that strives to move forward every day and keeps climbing to help me achieve my goals in business and my personal life.

I have known Peter Cox for almost seven years and I made the decision to engage Peter in my business over 18 months ago. This was one, if not the best decision I have made in business!

Peter has an amazing ability to get to the core of an issue and see things from a different perspective. One of the main things Peter has taught me about being successful is that I need multiple streams of revenue to have sustainability and this is why in 2017 I found premises and started my second business, Braeside Joinery. Both businesses are running successfully; this again is hugely due to Peter's leadership in helping me grow my culture in the business. In a short period of time Braeside has gone from doing small renovation jobs to building multi-million-dollar luxury homes and undertaking large commercial projects. I have a solid team and a good working environment for all my staff which allows them to deliver consistency in quality and on time."

**— Ross Cummings, Owner and Founder,
Braeside Building**

"Just here for a moment to have a talk to you about the great work that Peter Cox has done with the team over the last eight years, and the work he has done with our leadership groups. From an interesting point of view for me is that leaders are very important because not only do they have to lead on the field, they have to lead off the field for us so that we can all stay on the same page and keep our work ethics and our mental toughness together. So, having Peter work with the groups as individuals and then as groups is something that we've really relied on and has become essential to our performance. A lot of people say that leaders are born; that could be true – I think every person has a leadership trait or a leadership quality. But I think the ability to hone those traits and qualities and then have them brought out of the person and have that person transition those skills to his fellow players, that's the 1%, that's that little bit extra that Peter Cox brings to us and he has done a fantastic job – we've made three grand finals and won two premierships and the evidence of his work is there for all of us

to see. I don't think we have to go much further than that, if you ever want to have a look at Peter's work just pick up one of those grand finals and have a look at that."

— Donny Singe, Head of High Performance,
Manly Warringah Sea Eagles NRL Team

Sources:

1. www.smithsonianmag.com/history/the-daredevil-of-niagara-falls-110492884/
2. www.americanheritage.com/blondin-hero-niagara

CHAPTER 6

Nothing can grow and you'll never succeed when division exists. Relationships that are broken break because of division, and division is disunity. The "U" in FLITU is for unity (which I covered in Chapter 2) and if you don't have it you will never, ever replace yourself in your business and it ultimately could see you lose your business.

Growing unity is a huge driving force for Leadership Dynamics to grow the right people and the right behaviours around the business owner.

Having been in business for myself since 1988, we have experienced division and disloyalty, which ultimately is disunity. One thing that can really hurt you in life is people, and no doubt you too have experienced division and disloyalty in your life.

Over my years to date in business, I have witnessed close friends and clients become derailed by disunity and division.

Nothing can grow with division and disunity and you'll never replace yourself in the business. Ever. There needs to be a deliberate process to strengthen unity and grow it. It won't just happen by itself.

Who has been disloyal to you?

Who is creating division in your life?

Here's my version of a true story I've read on just how devastating even well-meaning disunity can be ...

Whhhuuummpp! An arrow pierced the cool night air of the Swiss camp in the village of Arth, landing at the feet of the leader of the Confederates. Fearing an imminent attack, the rabble of the peasant army quickly drew their crude weapons while seeking cover, steadying themselves to fight for their lives and awaiting orders.

However, no further arrows followed. Upon further inspection of the lone arrow, a note was found, bound tightly to its length.

It was a warning from one of the enemy, a Habsburg knight by the name of Henry Huenenberg, who recognised the superiority of his force and (possibly) thought that victory over such a lesser opponent would be a massive disgrace to his knightly code. So, in an act of absolute chivalry, he warned the peasant army that the Habsburg forces (3,000–5,000 of heavily armoured, well-trained knights) were not going to attack the Village of Arth as the Confederates thought, but were instead plotting to advance through Morgarten and that the peasants should return to their homes.

However, as history witnessed at the end of the thirteenth century, the Confederates were not deterred from their vision of maintaining their freedom and their lands from the hands of the Austrians, despite being seemingly outmanned, unskilled, unarmoured and under-resourced. They instead planned a roadblock and an ambush at a point between Lake Agerisee and Morgarten Pass, where a small path led between a steep slope and a swamp. A perfect place for a surprise attack.

The unsuspecting and highly confident Austrian force, led by Leopold of Austria, approached the pass, completely unaware of what was about to unfold. Before they knew what hit them, the Confederate army attacked from above – throwing rocks and logs headlong onto knights and coming at them with halberds. Whoever wasn't clonked on the head by a rock or log, was forced into the swamp and killed by the peasant army.

A great day for the Swiss. Not so much for the Austrians. And all because of a little note attached to an arrow from one very well meaning and extremely chivalrous Austrian knight, Henry Huenenberg. History's pages could have read so vastly different if that arrow hadn't been shot into the Confederate camp all those centuries ago. [1]

One little act of disunity unravelled the plans of a vastly superior Austrian army of knights versus a band of untrained, unarmoured, outnumbered and under-resourced, but highly unified, band of Swiss peasants …

As I'm sure you can appreciate, and have no doubt discovered for yourselves, unity plays the most pivotal role in the success of a team and business. No unity, no success. You and your team are destined to go headlong into the swamp, like Leopold and his burly knights, without it, so if you want to achieve your vision, you as the leader and business owner must work constantly at building a team around you that's unified and totally committed to the vision. End of story.

Do you have disunity within your business?

I've had the honour and privilege to implement my Leadership Dynamics process with elite sporting teams and many corporate organisations and businesses to lead them for growth, building their culture and leading them to develop a unified and harmonious team.

When I first meet new clients, there are always unity and harmony issues, but when properly implemented, the Leadership Dynamics process will give you a winning team culture and build a harmonious and unified team to give you outstanding results and allow you to eventually replace yourself in the business.

Unity and harmony require the heart and spirit of individuals to be aligned with trusting relationships and require individuals to believe in themselves and each other. Chapter 5 focussed on this.

On the 23 May 1953, 11:30 a.m., Edmund Hillary and Tenzing Norgay reached the top of Mount Everest, the highest mountain peak in the world. They were part of the British Everest expedition team assembled by Colonel John Hunt, comprising eleven climbers, a filmmaker and a physiologist. The preparation for a climb of this magnitude is huge – months of planning, training as a team, building trust and belief in each other to reach the summit, and facing some of the most extreme weather, altitude and terrain on the planet. Besides having the physical and technical abilities to climb the summit, it was critical that the team had immense belief and trust in themselves. [2]

While most of us will never climb Mount Everest and literally put our lives in the hands of others, we will however, if we want to develop a high-performing, unified and harmonious team, need to face our own Mount Everests, and will need to develop high levels of trust and belief within our teams. Without belief and without trust, you cannot create unity and harmony.

You only need one person to believe in you in life and you can do great things. When belief is built into people, when they're built up, it's incredible what they're capable of.

It's a leader's responsibility to inspire and breathe belief into the people they lead to become more than they currently are. When we build belief, it sparks in individuals the drive to want to become more and it grows high-performance teams.

What are you doing to empower and grow belief in the people you surround yourself with?

Do the people you surround yourself with believe in you as the owner and leader?

Who builds self-belief into you?

There are a number of key strategies I use within my Leadership Dynamics process that I implement to grow belief so that you can build unity and harmony and ultimately replace yourself in the business. In this chapter I'll outline a few of these highly effective strategies.

The Right People for the Right Roles

One of the very first strategies I implement when I enter a new client's business is to determine the different personalities of the key people in the business, using a personality profiling test.

When you truly understand a person's personality type, it gives you incredible perspective and insight into each of your key people, which allows you to lead them in a way that their personality will respond to the best, which will ultimately result in creating unity with you as the leader, and will nine times out of ten give you an outstanding performance.

Understanding the different personality types will also allow you to ensure that you place the right people in the right roles. There are definitely some personality types that are better suited to accounting, for example, than to upfront leadership, or to human resources than to sales. When you have the right people in the right roles, according to their personality type and strengths, you create unity as people will thrive in and enjoy their positions. When you place the wrong people in the wrong roles, you create disunity and disharmony as your people will struggle to truly find their feet and perform well – affecting not only their happiness, but also the happiness of those around them.

Do you know your personality type?

Do you know the personality type of your key people?

Do you have the right people in the right roles?

Understanding Personality Strengths

The authenticity of building belief in people comes from you understanding what your strengths are, which will enable you to better understand the people you have around you and to grow them to their full potential – to grow their belief in themselves – which will unify the team you lead.

We spend too much time focussing on people's weaknesses that we too often neglect the power of discovering and focussing on the strengths of our people. Not surprisingly, people like to use the skills they're good at, and studies have found that when we place them in roles that allow them to do this, employee engagement and performance skyrockets. This also obviously grows unity and harmony within your business. Why? Because people feel engaged and empowered when they're truly contributing.

What are your personality strengths?

What are the personality strengths of the people you surround yourself with?

How are you utilising your team's personality strengths?

Do you have a process to determine and analyse what the key strengths of your key people are, and where best to use these strengths in your business?

Building Trust Using Edification to Grow Unity

A powerful two-pronged strategy that the Leadership Dynamics process focusses upon to build trust into the business to grow unity is edification:

"You can promote anyone but yourself".

Edification is rocket fuel to grow trust and unity.

Trust in your team is much more than your team catching you in a team-bonding exercise; it's a deep-down knowledge that each team member has your back – that each team member is extremely loyal and dependable in all circumstances.

Having this level of trust in your team allows team members to completely embrace each other and the vision, and this creates unity and harmony, as you're all pulling in the same direction.

Developing unity and harmony to build trust requires the heart and spirit of individuals within the team to be aligned and unified.

You as the business owner have the most influence to build trust when you publicly and privately edify individuals purely from your heart. It cannot be fake and manipulative, or you will lose trust, not gain it, because you're not authentic and therefore you dilute your influence. People know when you're sincere or not.

When you edify individuals privately or when you edify individuals in public in front of their peers in relation to the strengths they bring to the organisation, it escalates trust and strengthens unity and harmony.

Edification is working on the heart and spirit of individuals and you will start to build trust rapidly within the team you lead when you do it.

Edification is high-level leadership that helps you to grow your business and replace yourself.

When is the last time you've edified someone?

Do you have an effective edification process in your business?

Trust via Transparency

If you want to build the heart and spirit of individuals in your team, you need to lead with transparency, as through transparency, you're going to earn trust and therefore, you'll ultimately build unity.

A colleague relayed a true story late last year about a family member who's a team leader in a large corporation. She was explaining how she'd recently put herself forward for a promotion at work and knew she was the most qualified candidate. However, she didn't get the job. Another team leader did. She found out quickly through the grapevine that the reason she didn't get it was due to another team leader going on extended leave and they needed her to cover the other team too, otherwise they'd have two large teams without leaders for 12 months. Not good for business, but this team leader understood this and said she would've made the same decision.

But what she found incredibly disappointing was that upper management hadn't explained this; and they weren't transparent. All they had been doing, in her words, were:

"Sucking up to me so I stay. They didn't give me the respect as a team leader and explain the truth behind the decision. They didn't trust me to understand or agree".

You can see the damage that was done through lack of transparency and no public or private edification of her contribution to the business and team player spirit, which was never acknowledged.

Are you transparent with the people you lead?

Are you edifying the right people?

Are you growing trust which grows unity?

Trust via Loyalty

The word "loyalty" conjures up many an image in our minds – from the lone soldier risking his own life by carrying his critically injured mate through a war zone to safety, to Lassie the wonder dog never leaving his master's side to, on the flip side, broken loyalty when a life partner walks out the door, never to return.

The media of late seems to be full of stories of sportspeople breaking contracts and leaving their club for another that will pay more money, and many people change jobs every one to two years in search of a better offer. Divorce rates are around one in two marriages, and the online world constantly bombards us with a myriad of images, offers and choices allowing us, with the click of a button, to try something, or someone, new. It's so tempting. It's so easy.

Loyalty is a key factor in developing trust to build unity and you need to give real loyalty to get real loyalty. When I lead people, I've got to give my loyalty if I want to get loyalty back. When I give loyalty, I'm starting to build trust by earning loyalty.

I'm starting to truly show people that I believe in them and that I trust them. You have to give trust to gain trust. When you do this, people feel valued. It makes them feel heard and it makes them feel special, and as a result, you build unity.

> *"People don't care how much you know until they know how much you care."*
>
> **— Theodore Roosevelt**

The Leadership Dynamics process grows loyalty, trust, belief, and transparency, making people feel valued, which means making people feel the owner truly cares about them. This results in a united team, so you can replace yourself in the business as the owner.

How are you growing loyalty?

Do you have loyalty?

If you don't have loyalty, why not?

The Pareto Principle

The Pareto Principle is named after the Italian economist, Vilfredo Pareto, who found that the 80/20 distribution occurs extremely frequently across the board in many situations. For example, in general, 80% of your sales come from 20% of your customers. And when you apply this principle to your team, 80% of your achievements and progress will come from 20% of your team. Therefore, as the leader, you need to know who your top 20% is and spend 80% of your time with them.

Who is the top 20% of your team that you cannot afford to lose?

You need to ensure there's unity and harmony among these top people. If you don't get unity and harmony because trust or belief breaks down, it leads to poor productivity, ineffectiveness of leadership, lost opportunity and lost momentum, and if they're responsible for 80% of your business success, then you're in real trouble.

Effective leaders understand the importance of the people they surround themselves with. If you strengthen trust between your key people – your top 20% (at the very least) – which results in strengthening unity and harmony within the leadership team, it will create momentum because you are creating a high-performance team. This, in turn, leads to the results you want to achieve and enables you to replace yourself in the business.

Growing unity never stops.

Assume nothing!

The moment you think you have unity, division's coming and effective leaders have processes in place to discern disunity and dividing behaviours and prevent them with proactive leadership. Division and disunity will tear your business and your life apart.

Disunity and division results in hurt and pain and it leads to major disruption and sometimes catastrophic repercussions and it must never ever be assumed that the team you're leading and the business you own are completely unified. The more people you have in your business, the greater the risk of disunity and division.

The Leadership Dynamics process implements a number of key strategies to grow unity, of which only a few have been outlined in this chapter, but I know this chapter has highlighted the sheer importance of continually focussing on unity and having deliberate strategies and processes within your business to build it.

"Peter's passion for leadership, his guidance and him being a dreamer and visionary has helped us to understand the basic leadership principles and how to utilise these principles. He has provided us with the tools and skills to keep moving our business in the right direction. Peter's desire and enthusiasm to grow people and organisations is exemplary.

He has influenced us in many areas of our lives including our personal life as well as growing our business to a successful level. We've had a lot of challenges along the way in growing our business and Peter has helped us tackle these head on and to constantly overcome obstacles and take action in a forward motion. Most importantly he has taught us to grow ourselves in order to be the best individuals we can be to enable us to grow in other areas in our life. The impact Peter Cox has had on our life:

– He taught us to DREAM BIG and believe in ourselves without losing sight of who we are and keeping true to our values and doing right by people along the way on our journey to success.

– Peter has equipped us with the essential skills required to build our business and lead people, very important especially in business.

– Most empowering of all, he has taught us that in achieving success and growing ourselves, you can also remain happily married through what can often be a very challenging journey.

– Peter Cox walks the talk; he is a man who leads by example and practices what he teaches. This is a very rare quality.

– His values, honesty, integrity and loyalty to the team give you the utmost confidence in working with him.

– He is a visionary, a man who knows where he's going and how to get there and in such a manner that you can be proud and hold your head high at the end of the day."

**— Stan and Leila Sithole, Co-Owners,
Urban Fitness Solutions**

Sources:

1. en.wikipedia.org/wiki/Battle_of_Morgarten
   www.warhistoryonline.com/medieval/battle-morgarten.html
2. www.nationalgeographic.com/adventure/features/everest/sir-edmund-hillary-tenzing-norgay-1953/

Summing Up

Most business owners who start the long journey of owning their own business dream of wealth and freedom. That's been my personal experience meeting with many business owners since I first went into business for myself all those years ago.

The business shouldn't need you – replace yourself in 180 days.

What this means is choice. It doesn't mean you're selling your business, or you have no role in your business. Every business owner has different needs and the one common denominator when I meet business owners is that they want quality time with their families to do the things they love doing in their life.

Some business owners want to work four days a week, while others want to work three days a week. Some want only to be at a Board meeting once a month.

For the needs of the business owner to be met when it comes to wanting more time, which means being replaced in the business so that the business doesn't rely on them, the six chapters of this book, which have outlined some of my Leadership Dynamics process, answer the following six questions to create a pathway to having the choice to replace yourself in your business.

1. *Who leads you?*
2. *Do you have influence?*
3. *What's your vision?*
4. *Have you set clear expectations?*
5. *Do you have a winning team culture?*
6. *Do you have unity and harmony?*

Any "noes" to the above six questions, and you won't replace yourself in your business.

Thank you for taking the time to read my book. I know it will stimulate and agitate you to replacing yourself in your business and living the life that you planned when you first started it.

Take care and all the best,
Peter

"I first met Coxey at an afternoon business function and I made the immediate decision to bring his Leadership Dynamics process into my business to grow my leadership and my leaders around me. Our relationship has grown with trust and respect and our leadership journey continues together positively impacting my life and my family's life. His powerful leadership process stimulates and agitates positive change quickly and leads to business and personal growth."

— Julian Fadini, Founder,
Bellevue Capital Financial Services and
Property 360

"I have been coached through Peter's Leadership Dynamics process for over three years. Peter's dynamic personality, strategic thinking style, and ability to challenge and motivate have been drivers in supporting my team's professional growth.

I particularly value Peter's direct approach and ability to get straight to the heart of any issue at hand. He will ask the right questions to help you to not only identify blockages, but also the actions required to remove those blockages preventing you from reaching your full leadership potential.

In the words of Peter himself, 'if your thinking doesn't change, nothing changes'. Peter's mentorship has challenged my thinking around leadership and empowered me with the tools to develop a strategic mindset, communicate more effectively, and to ultimately grow as a leader both professionally and on a personal level."

— Adriana Tsiailis, Associate,
Vobis Equity Attorneys

"Peter was introduced to me about five or six years ago by Des Hasler. Peter has shown me many different techniques to empower myself to do with Rugby League which has really helped as we've won two premierships during that time. I've also been able to use Peter's techniques in my personal life to improve my relationships, my communication and the confidence to be a good person, and to continue with my family life. I'd recommend Peter to anyone professional or personal. He's a great leader, and he's got my tick of approval."

— Matt Ballin, former player for Manly Warringah
Sea Eagles. Current Coach,
Manly Sea Eagles Jersey Flegg Team
Under 20s and, Education and
Wellbeing Officer, Manly Sea Eagles

Discover How to Replace Yourself in Your Business

Experience the choice and freedom owning your own business should bring

Since 2003, with his Leadership Dynamics business, Peter Cox has been working alongside small to medium sized business owners, CEO's, Company Directors and professional sporting organisations, sharing with them his 30+ years of global leadership experience and his proven processes and strategies to grow thriving businesses and teams and to help them live better lives.

Peter's Leadership Dynamics process has been a significant contributor to the growth of his corporate and business clients, some achieving up to 1000% growth over a 10-year period.

Discover the Leadership Dynamics Process so you can replace yourself in your business and experience the choice and freedom you desire!

For more information, visit

www.leadershipdynamics.com.au